Who Wants PIZZA?

The Kids' Guide to the History, Science & Culture of FOOD

Jan Thornhill

SCHOLASTIC INC.
New York Toronto London Auckland
Sydney New Delhi Hong Kong

Scholastic is constantly working to lessen the environmental impact of our manufacturing processes.
To view our industry-leading paper procurement policy, visit www.scholastic.com/paperpolicy.

Design by Jan Thornhill.

Text copyright © 2010 by Jan Thornhill.
All rights reserved. Published by Scholastic Inc., 557 Broadway, New York, NY 10012,
by arrangement with Owlkids Books Inc.
Printed in the U.S.A.

ISBN-13: 978-0-545-48420-6
ISBN-10: 0-545-48420-0

11 12 13 14 15   40   21 20 19 18 17 16

Contents

Who Wants Pizza?

I do!

And probably you do, too,

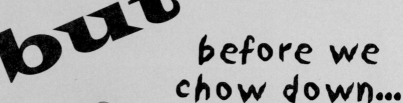 before we chow down...

...maybe we should ask some questions about...

FOOD

Why do we need to eat?

Where does our food come from?

Is there enough food for everyone?

Are some food choices better than others?

Why Eat?

Every living thing on Earth needs energy to survive. This energy can come from only one place — the Sun.

Plants use the Sun's energy to convert carbon dioxide into sugars through the process of photosynthesis.

Animals get the Sun's energy by eating plants, by eating animals that eat plants, or by eating animals that eat plant-eating animals.

Who Eats What?

Herbivores

Herbivores get all their energy from the plants they eat. Many herbivores, like tortoises, can eat a wide variety of plant matter. Others have evolved into such picky eaters that they are dependent on a single food. Australian koalas are so stuck on eucalyptus leaves that zoos in other countries have to fly their food in!

Carnivores

Carnivores are meat eaters. To get the fresh supplies of meat they need, most carnivores are predators and actively hunt their food. Carnivores have special skills, such as speed and agility, and special body parts, such as sharp teeth and hooked beaks, that make them successful hunters.

Omnivores

Omni means "all" — so to be an omnivore means you can eat all things. Lots of animals are omnivores. Many mammals and birds, such as bears and robins, will eat a wide variety of plant and animal matter. But some animals stretch the limits of eating "all things." One of these is the rat. Another is the human. Humans are a successful species partly because we will eat almost anything. You name it — from spiders to tortoises, from sharks to caterpillars, from snails to rats — some human, somewhere, has eaten it.

What's So Good About Pizza?

Some people think of pizza as junk food, but if it's homemade with a variety of healthy ingredients, it's got everything your body needs.

Calories

The energy we get from the Sun by eating is measured in calories. The more active you are, the more calories your body needs. If you eat more calories than your body burns through exercise, the leftovers are converted into stored fat. Everything on a pizza has calories, but meat, cheese, and dough have way more calories than vegetables or pizza sauce.

Vitamins

The thirteen vitamins your body needs are called micronutrients ("micro" because they're so tiny). Each of these vitamins works in different ways to keep you healthy. Some dissolve in water, and others dissolve in fat. Because your body isn't very good at storing the water-soluble ones, like vitamin C, you need to eat a variety of nutritious foods every day to make sure you get enough of each. Every part of a pizza provides vitamins, but some ingredients, like vegetables, offer more than others.

Minerals

The fourteen minerals you need to keep healthy are also micronutrients, and like vitamins, each works in different ways. While you need only minute amounts of trace minerals, you need larger amounts of major minerals, such as calcium, which builds your bones and teeth and keeps them strong. A well-topped pizza should provide you with most minerals your body needs.

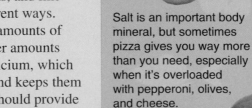

Salt is an important body mineral, but sometimes pizza gives you way more than you need, especially when it's overloaded with pepperoni, olives, and cheese.

Carbohydrates

Carbohydrates, made up of carbon and water, are turned into a sugar called glucose by your digestive system. Like gas in a car, glucose is your body's fuel. Sweet foods contain simple carbohydrates that are quickly absorbed into your bloodstream.

Starches in grains and potatoes are called complex carbohydrates and take a lot longer to break down into glucose. In a pizza, carbohydrates are mostly found in the starchy crust and in peppers, tomatoes, and pizza sauce.

Fats

Fats are needed by every cell in your body and are necessary for normal brain and nerve functioning. Extra fat can be used as body fuel or stored as...fat! Fats on a pizza come from cheeses and meats and oil in the sauce, dough, or olives.

Proteins

Proteins are the building blocks of your body and are made up of molecules called amino acids. Animal products are good sources. Other sources are grains, beans, nuts, and seeds, but these plant proteins lack some amino acids, so to get a complete protein, you have to combine them. Easy combos are peanut butter and bread, corn tacos and beans, or rice and soybean tofu. Protein on a pizza usually comes from cheeses and meats.

Do I Need Extra Vitamins?

If you eat a healthy, varied diet, you shouldn't need to take extra vitamins. But there are some exceptions. If you're a strict vegetarian, you probably don't get enough vitamin B_{12} because it's primarily found in animal products. Also, because our bodies make vitamin D from the Sun, it's now suggested that you take supplements, especially in the wintertime, if you spend little time outdoors, or live far from the equator.

9

How Do We Use Food?

Food wouldn't do you any good if your digestive system didn't break it down and extract the nutrients your body needs.

Open Wide

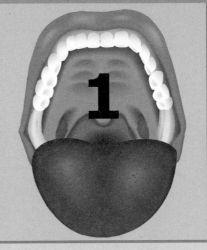

Before you take your first bite of food, glands in your mouth are already starting the digestive process by producing saliva. As you chew, saliva mixes with your food, making it slippery so it can slide easily down your throat. Enzymes and bacteria in your saliva begin to break down food before it even reaches your stomach. Other friendly mouth bacteria ward off attack from disease-causing microbes. There's such a zoo of bacteria in your mouth that more than 500 different strains have been identified that live just in the spaces between your teeth and gums!

Even before you take a bite of a burger, your digestive system has started to work.

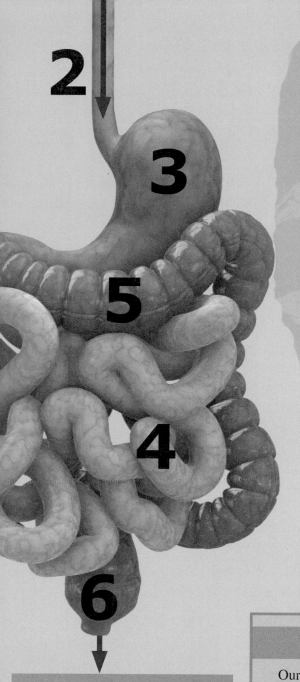

Inner Workings

2 When you swallow food, it slides down your esophagus, triggering a flap called the epiglottis to cover the entrance to your windpipe, or trachea, so food doesn't go down the wrong way and get into your lungs.

3 Strong muscles in your stomach churn and mash food into smaller pieces. At the same time, gastric juices help turn the food into a liquidy mess — that's what you see if you throw up. Your stomach then gradually empties that juicy mess into your small intestine.

4 The small intestine is a long tube packed into your gut. With some complicated help from your pancreas, liver, and gallbladder, the chunky stomach soup becomes thin and watery and nutrients are absorbed into your blood.

5 What's left is mostly watery waste that flows into your large intestine, a fat tube about as long as you are tall. When this waste reaches the colon, your body absorbs a few leftover minerals and a lot of water. This leaves you with solid waste you need to get rid of.

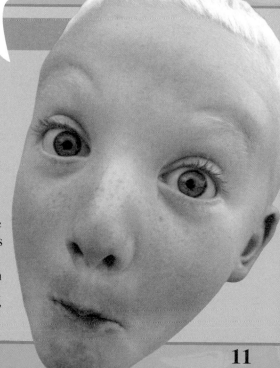

Honest, it was my gut flora!

The Way Out

6 The large intestine pushes the solid waste — let's just call it what it is: poop — to the last stop of the digestive system, the rectum. The poop stays there until you "need to go." That's when you sit on the toilet and push the poop through the outside opening of the rectum, called the anus. Don't forget to flush!

It Wasn't Me!

Our bodies are made up of trillions of human cells, but in our guts alone there are ten times that number of living microorganisms that are definitely not human. Some of these microorganisms, or gut flora, break down indigestible compounds in our intestines. When they do this, they produce gases…gases that are sometimes smelly…gases that almost always want to escape. And then they do. So now you can say, "It wasn't me! It was my gut flora!"

Why We Like Pizza

Most of us like pizza because it looks good, it smells good, and it tastes good.

That Looks Yummy!

Humans are very visual animals, so it's no surprise that we often decide what to eat by what we see. The makers of processed foods know this. That's why color is so often on lists of ingredients — to make food look more appealing. Also, in one study, test subjects who could see their food ate much more than others who were blindfolded — but the blindfolded ones reported being just as full on less food!

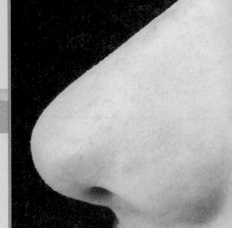

Did we evolve color vision to see the difference between ripe red fruit and inedible green leaves?

The Nose Knows

Your nose, not your tongue, is responsible for most of how you get a sense of complex flavors. You can prove this with an apple and an onion. Plug your nose and take a bite of each with your eyes closed. You won't be able to tell which is which until you unplug your nose!

Special Stinky Foods

People around the world have favorite stinky foods that other people find repellant. One of these is the prickly durian fruit. It tastes like almond custard but smells so bad it's been banned on some buses and trains in Singapore!

A Taste for Food

Our taste buds can sense five basic flavors: sweet, salty, bitter, sour, and umami. Sweetness steers us toward carbohydrate-rich foods, while a bitter taste encourages us to spit out poison. Vegetables are often a bit bitter, and since kids are more sensitive to bitterness than adults, most kids aren't big Brussels sprouts fans. Umami is used to describe a savory taste. Meat, cheese, and tomatoes are rich in umami — and all are ingredients that go on pizza!

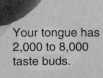

Your tongue has 2,000 to 8,000 taste buds.

ICK! YUCK! EW! GROSS!

Don't Eat That!

An inborn sense of disgust keeps us from eating things that might make us sick, but what disgusts us can vary greatly between cultures. There are, though, a few things — corpses, rotten meat, bodily secretions, and of course, feces (poop) — that pretty much everybody agrees no one should eat.

Toxins produced by rotting and moldy food can make you sick.

Monkey Toes, Bird Saliva & Bugs

Cocoons, fish skin, crayfish, and frog legs.

So what kinds of weird foods do people eat? Well, if it's not poisonous and it can be chewed, it's probably been eaten. Think scorpions, monkey toes, nests made of dried bird saliva, pig snouts, and over 1,200 species of insects! You've probably eaten at least one kind of insect without even knowing it. The crushed shells of cochineal scale insects make a red dye that is widely used in candies, yogurts, fruit drinks, and ice creams.

Crushed scale insects give us a red food dye.

I'll Have Two Erasers with a Side of Dirt, Please

Some people have a medical disorder called pica that makes them eat things that really aren't food: dirt, dust, glass, hair, pencil erasers, burnt matches, chalk. One sufferer was a man named Michel Lotito, who actually made a living from his pica by eating glass and metal in public. He even ate a Cessna airplane!

Some pica sufferers get minerals their bodies lack from the odd things they eat.

13

How It All Started

There hasn't
always
been
pizza...

...we used to eat everything

RAW

We ate raw fruit,

and meat,

and fish,

and even bugs.

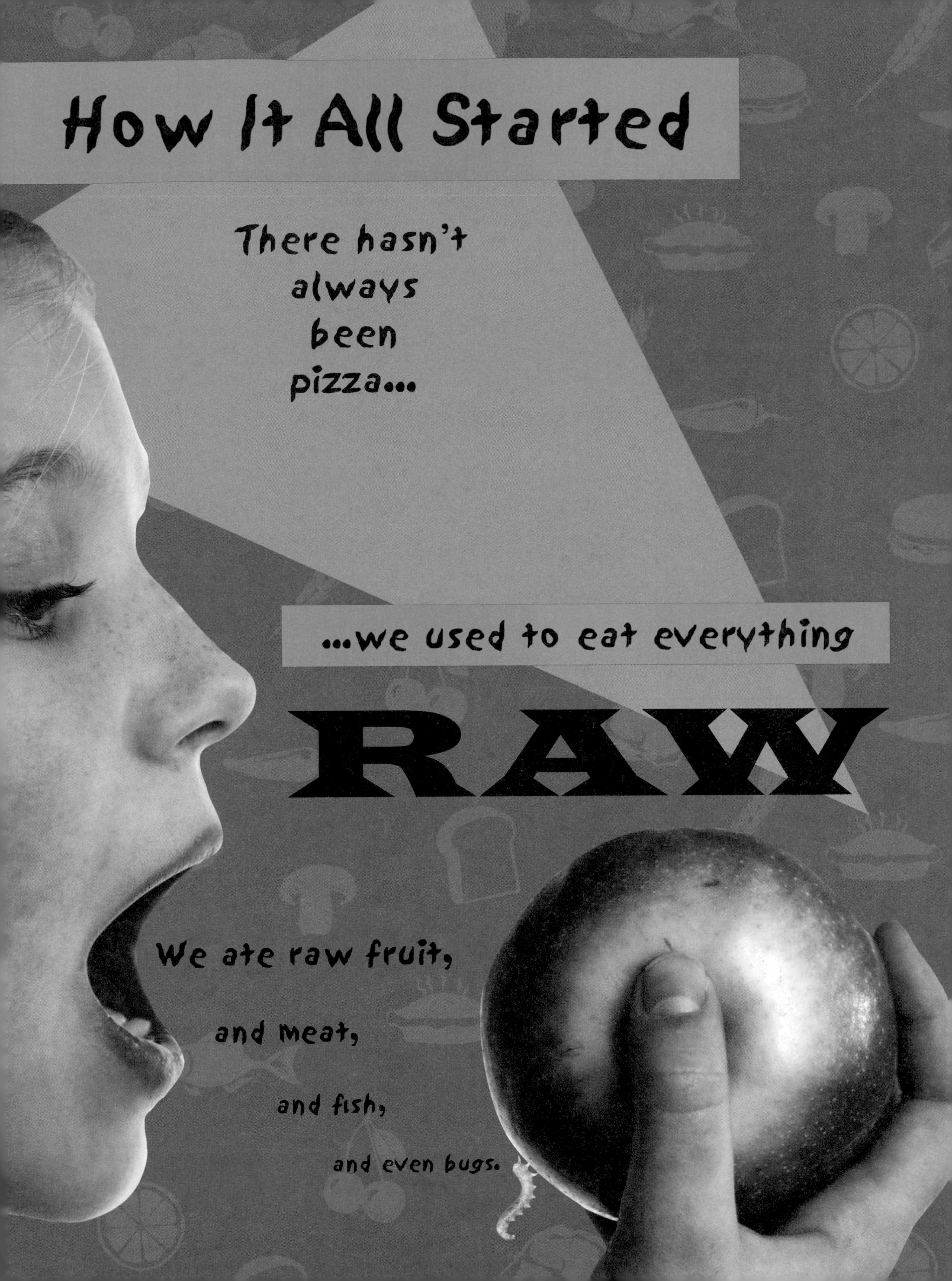

There was no flour for dough,
no tomatoes for sauce, and worst of all,
there was no cheese!

So how did we get from…

…raw meat…

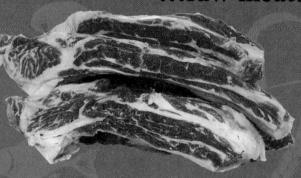

…to cooked?

From wild
grasses…

…to bread?

From dried fish…

…to frozen fish sticks?

Wild Harvest

For more than two million years, humans survived by hunting and gathering all their food from the wild.

Cave and rock art, like these carvings in Utah, give us clues to how ancient peoples hunted.

A Hard Life?

Hunting large animals with spears, digging roots and clams with sticks, climbing trees to gather fruits and eggs — this sounds like a lot more work than going to the grocery store and buying food. But hunter-gatherer societies, now and in the past, worked far fewer hours to provide for themselves than we do in modern society — between 15 and 20 hours a week!

Changing Together

Fossils show us that North American bison horns were once so long it would have been dangerous for the animals to live in herds. But once humans arrived and began hunting the bison, their horns gradually shortened and bison became herd animals. Hunting was good for both species. The bison provided food, clothing, and shelter for the hunters, and because the bison were forced by the hunters to move frequently, their prairie grasslands remained healthy.

A Varied Diet

Humans have evolved to eat a huge variety of foods. Our teeth can nibble or grind or tear and our jaws can work like a carnivore's or a herbivore's. Early on we discovered that in order to survive, we'd have to be willing to try all kinds of new foods — from nuts to roots to insects. This openness to experimentation survives today. That's why most of us are willing to try a juicy exotic fruit or a new flavor of chicken wings. It also might help explain why there are more than 1,400 different kinds of cheese in the world!

An African Bushman inspects a handful of delectable caterpillars.

Can I Eat This Berry?

We know that some plants are edible and others are poisonous. So how did we figure out what was safe to eat? By trial and error — taking a nibble of a new food and waiting to see what would happen. Early on we also figured out that many plant toxins, which protect plants against insect attacks, taste unpleasantly bitter, so we learned to avoid these. Interestingly, many of these bitter compounds have medicinal effects if taken in small amounts.

Liquid Gold

Honey is such a valuable source of calories, and tastes so good, that humans have braved painful bee stings for thousands of years to steal it from beehives. Eventually someone discovered that honeybees can be distracted with smoke, a technique that is still used by beekeepers today.

Following the flight of a honeyguide can lead to a wild beehive.

17

What's Cookin'?

Human beings are still the only animals that have learned to control fire.

ZAP!

A Lucky Strike

Early humans probably built their first fires using coals collected from the remains of blazes caused by lightning strikes. Captured fire provided warmth, protection from animals, and heat for cooking. Having light in the darkness of night also gave ancient people time to develop music, art, and storytelling — the very beginnings of civilization.

Fire = Bigger Brains?

About 1.8 million years ago, human brains suddenly grew much bigger. One scientist thinks this happened because we started cooking our food. Cooked food is much easier to digest. It's also much easier to chew. All this saved energy helped our brains grow. And because we no longer had to eat all day long, like some of our ape relatives do, we had more time to hunt, socialize, and invent tools.

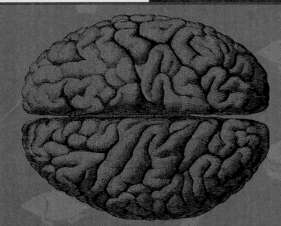

Up to 20% of the calories we take in are used for running our brains.

Sitting Around the Fire

Archeologists look for clues about prehistoric habits by studying bits of pottery, tools, and charred bones found near ancient hearths. One researcher found stone flakes left over from tool-making. These were puzzling because the type of stone used was too soft to make a useful item, though it chipped the same way as hard-to-find tool-stone would. What he figured out was that children must have been given the soft stone to practice making tools!

Hearths, or firepits, have been a social gathering place for hundreds of thousands of years.

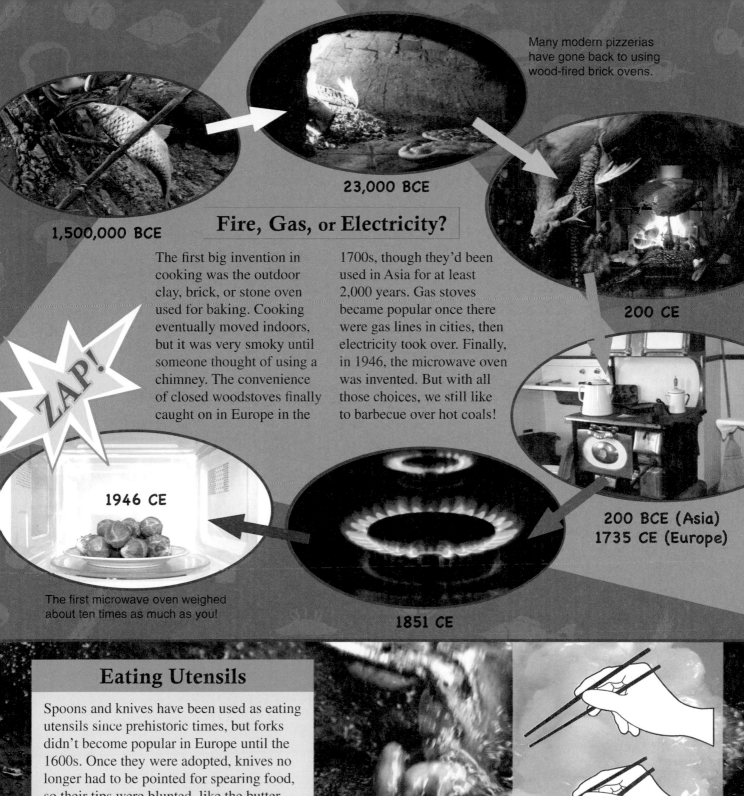

1,500,000 BCE

23,000 BCE

Many modern pizzerias have gone back to using wood-fired brick ovens.

200 CE

Fire, Gas, or Electricity?

The first big invention in cooking was the outdoor clay, brick, or stone oven used for baking. Cooking eventually moved indoors, but it was very smoky until someone thought of using a chimney. The convenience of closed woodstoves finally caught on in Europe in the 1700s, though they'd been used in Asia for at least 2,000 years. Gas stoves became popular once there were gas lines in cities, then electricity took over. Finally, in 1946, the microwave oven was invented. But with all those choices, we still like to barbecue over hot coals!

ZAP!

1946 CE

The first microwave oven weighed about ten times as much as you!

1851 CE

200 BCE (Asia)
1735 CE (Europe)

Eating Utensils

Spoons and knives have been used as eating utensils since prehistoric times, but forks didn't become popular in Europe until the 1600s. Once they were adopted, knives no longer had to be pointed for spearing food, so their tips were blunted, like the butter knives we use today. Chopsticks appeared about 5,000 years ago in China. Because there was a lack of firewood, food was cut into small pieces so it would cook quickly in a wok. No cutting was necessary at the table, so everyone used chopsticks.

If you can write with a pencil, you can master chopsticks.

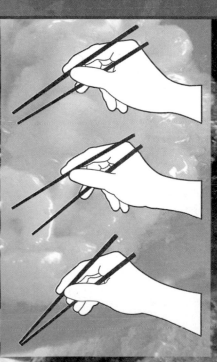

That's My Cow!

Domesticating wild animals gave us a constant source of food, clothing, and labor.

Domesticate: (v.) to selectively breed a species until it becomes accustomed to human care and control.

Tame: (v.) to train a *single* animal to become accustomed to human care and control.

How Was It Done?

Probably the first step in domesticating livestock was capturing baby animals and taming them. People would then have chosen to breed together the ones with the most desirable traits, such as calmness and trainability. Domestication was beneficial for the animals, too, since they were provided with food and protection from predators.

When Were They Domesticated?

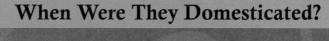

Cattle
Eastern Sahara

Pigs
Western Asia

Llamas
Peru

Horses
Kazakhstan

7500 BCE

3500 BCE

Goats
Western Asia

Honeybees
Egypt

9000 BCE

8000 BCE

6000 BCE

3000 BCE

Sheep
Western Asia

Chickens
Thailand

Camels
Saudi Arabia

20

Can We Domesticate Anything?

Out of almost 150 large herbivorous mammals, we've only managed to domesticate fourteen. To be a good candidate for domestication, an animal needs to possess a few important traits. It needs to be used to having a leader. It needs to be relatively calm. It needs to grow fast. And it needs to stay where you want it to. So don't expect to see domestic gazelles any day soon. They're way too skittish to keep in a pen. And rhinos and zebras? Uh-uh. They're just so bad-tempered and unpredictable, they're downright dangerous.

Water Buffalo
Pakistan

2500 BCE

Turkeys
Mexico

100 BCE

1500 BCE

1000 BCE

Geese
Germany

Reindeer
Siberia

From Animal to Meat

In earlier times, people usually knew the animals they were going to eat, so no one took their killing lightly. In fact, in many societies, people would take turns slaughtering animals so no one would become too used to it. It was also important that no part of an animal was wasted. Everything was used, from intestines to blood, from feathers to skin.

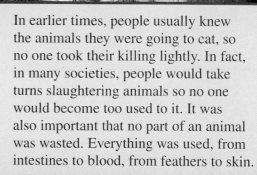

Black pudding is a sausage made of cooked blood and chunks of fat stuffed into cleaned intestines.

Dig! Plant! Reap!

About 10,000 years ago, people began to settle down in one place and plant seeds.

Putting Down Roots

As plants and animals were domesticated, people gave up hunting and gathering and became farmers. This change happened at least seven different times in different places, probably first in an area near the Mediterranean called the Fertile Crescent where many types of wild grains happened to grow.

Oats
Europe

2500 BCE

Rice
China

8000 BCE

Barley
Middle East

8000 BCE

Wheat
Middle East

8000 BCE

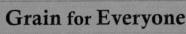

Grain for Everyone

Wild grains scatter their seed, but sometimes a mutant plant will hold its seed longer, making it easier to gather. By planting only seeds that didn't scatter, and by choosing the fattest ones and the ones that sprouted the most easily, we ended up with domesticated grains in only a couple of hundred years — grains that people around the world still depend on for the bulk of their food calories.

Corn
Mexico

7000 BCE

Millet
China

8000 BCE

Rye
Turkey

2000 BCE

Quinoa
Peru

4000 BCE

Plentiful Protein

People began domesticating legumes, a plant family that includes beans, peas, and lentils, around the same time as grains. Since wild legume seeds often explode from their distinctive pods when ripe, people looked for mutants that didn't split open easily. When eaten with grains, legumes make a complete protein, which has been important throughout history whenever animal protein was scarce.

The Beginning of Money

The first "money" was probably food — domestic animals or grains. Grain can be dried and stored, and it can be traded for other things if more is grown than needed. The earliest rich people would have been the ones with the most cattle or biggest stores of grain. Contents of graves tell us that as long as 5,000 years ago in China, there were already rich people and poor people.

When grains became too cumbersome as a unit of trade, silver coins were invented.

The Staff of Life

The first breads were simple and flat, made with only flour and water. Then someone discovered, probably by accident, that when yeast gets into dough the gases it produces make the bread light and airy. This might have happened when some dough was left long enough for wild yeast to start working on it or when someone mixed some yeasty beer into the dough instead of water.

Who Wants Spaghetti?

The world's oldest noodles, made in 2000 BCE from millet, were found in China. Italian wheat pastas were made by the ancient Romans, but there was no tomato sauce until 1839. Until then, people thought that the tomato Columbus had brought back from the New World was poisonous!

In earlier times, pasta was finger food.

Don't Let It Rot!

A big problem with fresh food is that it doesn't stay fresh very long. It goes bad. It rots. It smells.

All Dried Up

When foods are dried by the Sun or wind, the moisture-loving bacteria that break down dead things can no longer survive. Grain can last a very long time when dried like this, but fish and meat easily reabsorb moisture from the air and then go bad. Eventually, people figured out that salting, combined with drying, makes meat last longer.

Though dried food lasts, it doesn't taste fresh when you finally eat it.

Pickle Alchemy

Some bacteria can actually *help* food last and make it taste good, too. Under the right salty conditions, these bacteria produce sour lactic acid, beating out the bad bacteria that spoil food, in a process called fermentation. Traditional dill pickles are made this way, and so is sauerkraut and Korean kimchi. More modern pickles are made with vinegar.

Look Out, Bacteria!

Researchers think we started perking up our food with herbs and spices not so much for their taste, but because many of these flavorings are extremely effective bacteria killers. Even today, many people living in tropical areas can't afford refrigeration, but they continue to be protected by the spices they use in their food.

Garlic and onions top the list of super-killers of bacteria.

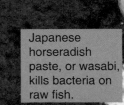
Japanese horseradish paste, or wasabi, kills bacteria on raw fish.

Can It!

In 1795, the French government offered a large reward for a method of food preservation to feed its armies. Fifteen years later — nearly fifty years before Louis Pasteur proved that heat kills bacteria — Nicolas Appert won the prize for his method of sealing food in glass bottles and boiling them. But it was the British who set up a factory and began selling food canned in tins to the public.

The can opener wasn't invented until 45 years after canned food was introduced!

Brrrrrr!

In 1912, an American named Clarence Birdseye learned from the Inuit in Canada that a fish frozen quickly can taste almost as good as fresh when it's cooked. Back at home, Birdseye's experimentation led to the birth of the frozen food industry, though it couldn't really take off until freezers became common in North American households in the late 1940s.

Modern Preservatives

The food industry now uses many different chemicals — including salt! — to stop the growth of bacteria and molds. These chemicals work well, though some people question their safety. A newer method of dealing with harmful bacteria is called irradiation, where foods are exposed to radiation energy. This energy destroys bacteria's ability to multiply.

This green symbol indicates that a food has been irradiated.

25

Don't Slurp!

Around the world, people have developed all kinds of different food rules, traditions, and recipes. Put together, these things become food culture.

Dos & Don'ts

As soon as we began eating together we began making rules about food — what you can eat, when you can eat it, and how you can eat it. People have rules about when you're allowed to snack, who gets to eat first, and whether or not you can burp at the table. These rules are always changing. For instance, in the not-so-long-ago past, cannibalism was practiced by many different societies, but today there is a universal taboo against it.

Let's Party!

Getting together to enjoy special foods began as a way to celebrate, and give thanks for, a successful hunt or harvest. As upper classes appeared, feasting became a way to show off wealth. Many people today still mark special occasions, such as weddings, birthdays, and religious holidays, by gathering together and sharing food.

At a single party in the 1500s, the queen of France served her guests 30 peacocks, 33 pheasants, 21 swans, 90 cranes, 66 guinea fowl, 30 capons, 90 hens, 99 quail, plus rabbits, hares, and pigs!

What's Wrong With This Picture?

Absolutely nothing...

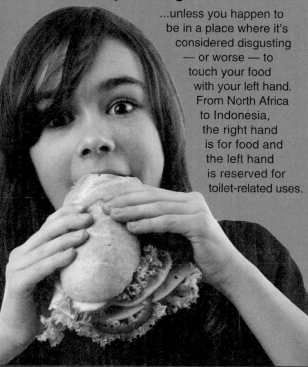

...unless you happen to be in a place where it's considered disgusting — or worse — to touch your food with your left hand. From North Africa to Indonesia, the right hand is for food and the left hand is reserved for toilet-related uses.

Cultural Customs

Different cultures have different food customs. A fifth of the world's population doesn't eat pork, and many Hindus don't eat *any* meat. In many places, food is eaten without utensils, and in countries that use chopsticks, it's very rude to point with them. In Russia, to show that your host has been generous, you're expected to always leave a little food on your plate, while in India and other places, it's impolite to leave anything at all.

Who Wants to Eat Out?

For a cheap, quick bite, street food is always a favorite.

China has a restaurant history that goes back a thousand years, but in Europe no one went out for meals until the rich were overthrown during the French Revolution. Aristocrats' chefs suddenly had no jobs, so they opened restaurants. Today, eating in restaurants, especially in fast food ones, is so popular that about half of America's food money is spent eating out! The original fast food is street food. From tacos in Mexico to noodle soup in Vietnam to pickled herring in the Netherlands, street snacks continue to be popular around the world.

I'll Try That!

People were once much more wary of trying foods from different cultures, but many of us today experiment with eating and cooking exotic recipes. This has created a huge market for cookbooks and imported foods, and has turned TV chefs into stars.

Eating out can be as basic as getting a pizza or as luxurious as dining in a Parisian restaurant.

Changing Food

Say you were born 5,000 years ago and you wanted a...

Carrot

You'd get this:

Not this:

Yum!

So how did we get from a pale, gnarly, bitter root to a sweet, juicy orange carrot?

And how did we get from:

A wild boar...

...to a pink pig?

From milk...

...to ice cream?

From real berries...

...to really *unreal* berries?

Eat Your Veggies!

How did our ancestors change wild plants into the fruits and vegetables we eat today?

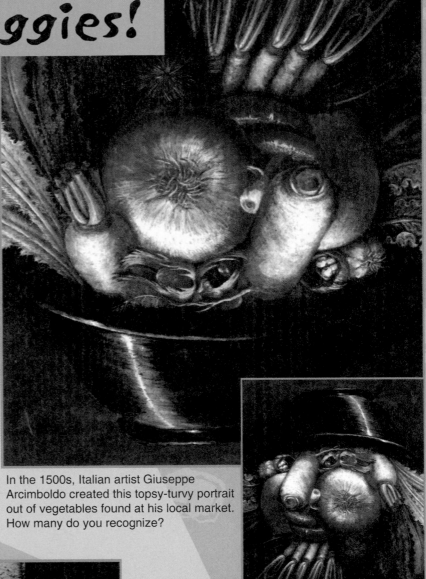

Wild Carrots Aren't Orange

Most of our vegetables today don't look a lot like their wild ancestors. Many, such as the carrot, were originally very bitter and tough. Once in a while, though, a plant would grow a slightly sweeter root, or it would be a bit more yellow, or a bit juicier than its parent. When the seeds of these plants were grown and selectively bred over the years — *voila!* — the sweet orange carrot we know today was born.

In the 1500s, Italian artist Giuseppe Arcimboldo created this topsy-turvy portrait out of vegetables found at his local market. How many do you recognize?

We can thank women through history for many of the foods we eat today.

Early Natural Scientists

The process of selecting and saving seeds from the best plants made early farmers the first natural scientists. Though they couldn't have known what we now do about genetics, they *did* know that their selection process could change the character of plants. Most of these early seed-savers were women, and in many cultures it's still women who select and gather food-plant seeds, and then share them with others.

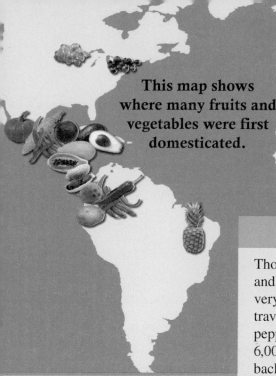

This map shows where many fruits and vegetables were first domesticated.

Where'd It Come From?

Though most of our vegetables and fruits were domesticated in very small areas, many have now traveled around the world. Chili peppers, first grown in Ecuador 6,000 years ago, were brought back to Spain by Columbus.

People loved the peppers' heat, and they quickly spread east. Chili peppers are now so connected to Thai, Indian, and Szechuan cooking that it's hard to believe these cuisines have been using them for less than 500 years!

First Fertilizer

Seabirds, like these blue-footed boobies, produce guano.

Fertile soil produces bigger and better crops, but growing food in the same soil year after year uses up nutrients. Early on, people figured out that one of the best ways to improve soil is to add animal waste, or manure, that's easily collected from domesticated animals. Another huge source was seabird droppings, or guano, that had built up over the years on island nesting grounds.

Mr. Mendel's Peas

One of the genetic traits Mendel looked for in pea plants was height.

People have always noticed that children inherit traits, or characteristics, from their parents, but at first they didn't know how. Gregor Mendel, an Austrian monk, began to find some answers in the mid-1800s. By breeding garden peas, he figured out that traits that are passed down from one generation to the next come in pairs — one from each parent. He also found that one of these traits has dominance over the other, and that some traits can skip generations. Though his "natural laws of heredity" were not recognized when he was alive, Mendel is now called the Father of Modern Genetics.

31

On the Farm

Over thousands of years, we've changed our farm animals so much that many breeds wouldn't survive if we set them free.

Oink!

All domestic pigs are descendants of the wild boar, a hairy, tusky brown animal that still roams free in forests today. Early farmers selectively bred variances in color in pigs, since a pink or black-and-white pig would be less camouflaged if it escaped. They also bred them to keep piglet traits, including tameness and shorter snouts and tusks.

Birds of a Feather

Domesticated jungle fowl, or chickens, probably were first bred for cockfighting. But their use for eggs and meat was not ignored. In 1400 BCE, the Chinese had already invented warmed incubators to hatch eggs. By the Middle Ages, there were three main types of chickens in Europe and Asia. But it wasn't until the 1800s that breeding really took off and exhibiting strange-looking chickens became a fad. Through selective breeding, meat chickens today grow three times as fast as they did only sixty years ago!

Meat or Milk?

The ancestor of almost all domestic cattle was the Aurochs, a humongous beast with huge horns. For thousands of years after domestication, cattle were multipurpose animals, used for milk, meat, and labor. Today we breed dairy cattle to produce milk and beef cattle for meat. Most beef cattle start their lives in fields but later go to feedlots, where many are fattened on corn. Cows are not designed to digest corn, and many people think that grass-fed beef is healthier for us to eat.

Crazy Numbers

Quick! What's the most numerous large mammal on Earth? Humans win, with 6.8 billion. And second? Cattle take the prize, with a population of 1.3 billion. Third are sheep, at 1.1 billion. And then come pigs and goats. All domesticated. To get what we want from these animals, we have made them the next most populous large mammals on the planet. But in trade for being fed and protected from predators, most are denied the freedom to live according to their instincts — to be active, to socialize, to choose mates, and to rear young.

Just a few of the world's 1.1 billion sheep.

125 Horsepower

2 Horsepower

0.1 Horsepower

Working Animals

We've bred lots of animals to work for us: horses, water buffalo, camels, dogs. For centuries, oxen, or trained cattle, did most of the heavy work on farms, since they were cheaper to keep than horses, and you could eat them. Work horses took over in the 1800s, when new farm equipment was developed that didn't fit oxen. By 1915, there were more than 21 million horses in the United States, but as gas-powered vehicles and farm equipment took hold, their numbers plummeted.

33

Scales & Fins

Fishing methods have improved so much in the past fifty years that some stocks are running out.

Fish On!

Though we've been fishing for over 100,000 years, we've only recently put a serious dent in fish populations. And no wonder, since we now have trawlers that drag the sea bottom with nets the size of soccer fields, and factory ships that can process 350 tons of fish a day!

A Lot of Fish

More than 100 million tons of fish and other sea creatures are caught in the world each year, providing us with about 15% of our animal protein. We eat a huge array of seafood, including eels, octopuses, and sea cucumbers. In Japan, people even eat a poisonous pufferfish. If it's not properly prepared by a licensed chef, it can kill you!

Fish Farming

Fish farming, or aquaculture, now provides half of the world's fish. It seems like a great way for us to get protein, but there are a few problems with it. Some farmed fish, such as salmon, have to be fed large amounts of feed made from wild fish. Waste is often released into surrounding waters, as are parasites and diseases that can affect wild fish stocks.

Bycatch

An incredible number of lives are wasted by fisheries to bycatch, or non-target species that are caught alongside the ones fishermen are trying to catch. A number of years ago, consumers demanded that tuna be caught in a way that didn't kill dolphins as bycatch. So the tuna fishery changed. Unfortunately, while the new method saves dolphins' lives, the bycatch is now much greater and includes large numbers of sea turtles, sharks, and other fish, many of which are actually threatened with extinction, unlike the dolphins.

Dolphins' lives are being saved, but at what expense?

The bycatch of shrimp fisheries can be five times the weight of the shrimp caught.

A Lifeless Ocean?

The world's oceans are a vast ecosystem that we're only beginning to understand. But we've been harvesting marine life as if there's a never-ending supply. There isn't. Some fisheries have already collapsed, and many others are being fished to their limits. Pollution is another huge problem, but the effects of climate change are probably the most important. If we don't come up with international agreements to solve these problems, the future of all ocean life may be in jeopardy.

Some scientists say that 90% of the oceans' large fish are already gone.

You Can Help!

Learn everything you can about the oceans and tell other people. Better yet, become a marine biologist! If you're going to eat seafood, try to find out whether or not it came from a properly managed fishery. Choose wild Pacific salmon instead of tuna or tiger shrimp. Most important, learn about and fight global warming, which is the largest threat — not just to our oceans but to our way of life.

35

Moo Juice

If someone, somewhere, didn't decide to try milking a cow or a goat, we wouldn't have cheese on our pizza!

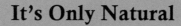

It's Only Natural

Though human milk is best for humans, all milk is nourishing, so we probably started milking other animals as soon as we domesticated them. Most babies produce an enzyme called lactase that allows them to digest milk sugar, or lactose. Long ago, no adults produced this enzyme, so they couldn't tolerate milk. Amazingly, though, in societies that have consumed dairy products for many years, a gene mutation allows many adults to continue to produce lactase so they can digest milk all their lives.

We've milked most domesticated animals, including camels and yaks.

Milking

For thousands of years, milking was done by hand, so dairy farmers couldn't keep up with more than one or two dozen cows. But then automatic milking machines were introduced and dairy herds grew. Today, a large dairy farm can manage hundreds of cows, and each cow can produce more than 100 glasses of milk a day!

Who Wants Cheese?

Cheese-making is a clever way to preserve the goodness of milk, which spoils quickly. In dairy-eating cultures, cheese is so popular that there are more than 1,400 different kinds, each one with its own unique character. There are fresh cheeses, hard cheeses, stinky cheeses, and cheeses riddled with mold. And there are some really strange cheeses, like Italian *casu marzu*. Considered a delicacy, it gets its distinct flavor from the digestive excretions of maggots!

The French make about 500 traditional cheeses.

Some cheeses are given unique flavor by fly larvae.

While most cheeses are pressed, mozzarella is stretched while it's being made, which gives it its characteristic stringiness when it melts.

Who Screams for Ice Cream?

People around the world have made chilled desserts for thousands of years, sometimes climbing mountains to get the ice they needed! But true ice cream, made with a hand-cranked device that used ice mixed with salt to freeze flavored cream, didn't show up until the 1800s. Today, ice cream is made by whipping air into the ice cream mixture as it's frozen.

Soy Products

For people who are lactose intolerant, or who want to eat fewer animal products, there are healthy alternatives made from soy beans. Lots of people drink soy milk, made by soaking ground soy beans in water, then boiling the filtered liquid. Tofu, or bean curd, originated in China about 2,000 years ago. It's made by curdling soy milk and then pressing the solids into a high-protein, cheese-like cake.

Making It All Taste Good

Though a fresh tomato can be delicious on its own, it's even tastier with a dash of salt, a splash of oil, and a bit of spice.

The Search for Flavor

World exploration was driven by a search not for gold or even land but for spices. So why were cloves, cinnamon, and black pepper so valuable? First, spices livened up a dull European diet and preserved food. Also, the Arabs who controlled the overland spice trade from the Far East had upped their prices, making spices fabulously expensive, which of course made them a status symbol. Unfortunately, this hunger for spices came at a cost to many of the peoples who grew them. As sea routes to the Far East and the Americas were discovered, one spice-growing nation after another was conquered and then controlled by foreigners.

Hot Stuff

Hot chili peppers get their heat from a chemical called capsaicin. It doesn't cause tissue damage in your mouth; instead, it triggers nerve receptors that your brain translates into a burning sensation. A protein in milk acts like a detergent on capsaicin, so the best way to lessen the heat is to take a swig of milk or nibble on some cheese.

Herbs & Spices

Herbs are the leafy green parts of aromatic plants, while spices are the harder parts — seeds, roots, or bark. Both get their unmistakable aromas and flavors from volatile oils. "Volatile" means evaporates easily, so freshly dried herbs and spices are much stronger, both in smell and in taste, than older stale ones.

The salt we use comes from mines, evaporated sea water, or salt plains, like this one in Bolivia.

Flavor Enhancers

All living things need salt to survive, which is probably why we humans like the way it perks up the flavor of food. But too much salt can cause health problems, and most of us, because we eat a lot of processed and restaurant foods, consume more than twice as much salt as our bodies need! MSG, or monosodium glutamate, is another flavor enhancer. It adds the fifth taste, umami, to food and is widely used in the food industry.

Mmm...Fat

Who doesn't like french fries, creamy Caesar dressing, a juicy cheeseburger, or a chocolate sundae? Guess what they all have in common? They're all high in fat! Each of us needs fat for our bodies to function properly, but too much fat, and some *types* of it, are bad for us. About a hundred years ago, a method called hydrogenation was discovered that makes fats last longer. These fats became popular in the processed food industry. Unfortunately, when liquid oils are hydrogenated, trans fats are created. Eating trans fats can increase the risk of heart disease.

One of the reasons we like whipped cream and chocolate is their fat content.

Natural & Artificial Flavor

yl acetate, amyl buty... ...l formate, benzyl aceta nzyl isobutyrate, butyric acid, cinnamyl isobutyrate, cinnamyl valerate, cognac ntial oi... ...tone, ethyl acetate, ethyl amyl ketone, ethyl b rate, e... ...tanoate, ethyl heptylate, ethyl lactate, ethyl thylphe... ...te, ethyl propionate, ethyl valerate, heliotrop droxyphe... ...nt solution in alcohol), a-ionone, isobutyl ant late, i... ...ssential oil, maltol, 4-methylacetophenone, met thranila... ...yl cinnamate, methyl heptine carbonate, methyl phthyl... ..., mint ess... ...l oil, ner

Why does an orange-flavored candy that has no orange juice in it taste like oranges? Food industry scientists recreate flavors using complicated mixtures of chemicals. Sometimes they extract these chemicals from nature. That's called "natural flavor" on labels. If they combine manufactured chemicals to create the same flavor, it's called "artificial flavor."

These hard-to-pronounce words are all chemicals found in artificial strawberry flavor.

ryl isobutyrate, orris butter, phenethyl alcohol, rose, rum ether, g-undecalact

Sweet Tooth

Try asking, "Who wants dessert?" I bet there won't be many people who answer, "Not me!" That's because humans have a soft spot for sweet things...and we always have.

Honeybees

The earliest source of sugar for humans would have been ripe fruit. But soon after came honey, collected from wild bees. About 5,000 years ago, we started luring honeybees into artificial hives. The honey could then be collected without harming the colonies. We also rely on domesticated bees to pollinate crops that produce about a third of all our food. Unfortunately, bees around the world are dying off in shocking numbers. No one's yet sure why, but this could be due to a lethal combination of infections, pesticides, lack of food, and genetic disorders.

Yummy Syrup

Native Americans were likely the first people to boil down sap from maple trees to make syrup, a sugar source that remained North America's main sweetener until the huge sugarcane industry took over. But then, in the late 1970s, a super-sweet syrup made by altering the natural sugars in corn became very popular. High-fructose corn syrup is cheap to make, so the food industry uses it in an astonishing variety of processed foods, from soft drinks to yogurts to breakfast cereals.

Maple sap is collected drop by drop.

Sugar's Not-So-Sweet History

Sugarcane, a tall grass from which white sugar is made, was brought to the Americas by Columbus. Local native field workers soon died from Old World diseases, so colonists began importing slaves from Africa to do the hard labor of producing sugar. About three-quarters of the roughly eleven million African slaves shipped across the Atlantic were forced to work making sugar — sugar that was used to sweeten the tea and cakes of Europeans and American colonists.

Candy

Ancient Egyptians made chewy concoctions by mixing fruit, nuts, and seeds with hot honey 3,500 years ago, so candy has a long history. But candy-making as we now know it, with all its variety, didn't really start until white sugar became readily available. Candy became so popular in America that there were 380 factories producing different types by the mid-1800s.

Happy Birthday!

Desserts of all sorts have been around for thousands of years...and so has the birthday cake! Even in ancient Greece, birthdays were celebrated with round cakes sweetened with honey. Candles first showed up on elaborate birthday cakes in Germany in the 1700s. Decorating birthday cakes with lit candles evolved into what we still do today — making a wish while blowing out the flames! Happy birthday!

Sort-of Foods

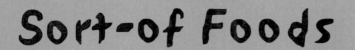

It can take time to make nutritious meals from scratch — and time is what many of us don't seem to have anymore.

New Eating Habits

Families used to sit down together three times a day to share home-cooked meals. But now, because of our hectic lives, we eat together as families less and less often. Most of us eat out at least once a week, and when we eat at home it's often pre-prepared or processed food.

Kids can consume more than half of their daily recommended calories in a single fast food meal.

High Sugar, Salt & Fat

Processed foods are foods that have been changed from their natural state. Milk, for example, is pasteurized to kill bacteria. Some foods, though, like cheese spread and fruit roll snacks, are so highly processed that they have little in common with their natural state. All kinds of things are added, such as flavors, colors, and thickeners. Some of the most common additives are fat, sugar, and salt. All three enhance flavor, but they can be unhealthy in the high amounts they're often used in processed foods.

Corn and soy beans are taking over! Not only are livestock fattened on them, but they're in almost all processed foods, showing up as oils, starches, flours, acids, glutens, lecithin, and high-fructose syrup.

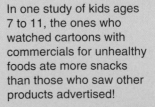

In one study of kids ages 7 to 11, the ones who watched cartoons with commercials for unhealthy foods ate more snacks than those who saw other products advertised!

Food: anything eaten that provides nutrition for the body.

Is It Food?

Many snack foods, soft drinks, and candy contain nothing your body can use other than calories. You fill up on them and feel like you've eaten, but you don't get the vitamins and minerals you would by eating more healthy food. If the main ingredients on food labels are fats, sugars (look for words that end in "ose"), and unpronounceable words, ask yourself this question before you eat it: Is it food?

Super-sizing

Have you ever noticed that you can sometimes eat incredible amounts of food you like? Early humans evolved an instinct to do this to take advantage of plentiful food because they often had none. Fast food marketers make more money when they take advantage of this human instinct by offering larger and larger servings of high-fat and high-sugar foods.

If you're not hungry enough to eat an apple…
…maybe you're not hungry!

- Drink water or fresh fruit juice instead of soft drinks.

- Try a bean burrito, pizza with veggies, or a grilled chicken sandwich instead of a burger and fries or chicken nuggets.

- Read labels and avoid hydrogenated fats, high-fructose corn syrup, high salt, and sugar.

- Mute commercials — read something until your show comes back on.

- Enjoy the taste of a crisp, juicy apple!

Scary Food

We can't live without food, but food can also be very dangerous. And some of our farming practices are not helping.

Avian influenza, or bird flu, spilled over from poultry to humans.

Zoonoses

Zoonoses — funny word! — are infectious diseases that can leap from non-human animals to humans. Diseases like measles, tuberculosis, flu, and the plague all originated in farm animals. And then they jumped to humans. These diseases didn't appear until we began living close to domesticated animals. Others, like the recent H1N1, continue to appear, and some say crowded factory farming is to blame.

What's in That Meat?

Salmonella and *E. coli* are bacteria that live in the digestive tracts of animals. Minute amounts of animal feces can contaminate food with bad varieties of these bacteria and make you ill. Millions of people are infected this way every year, and some even die. You can avoid becoming sick by washing your hands and kitchen tools after handling meat, and by killing bacteria with heat. Another foodborne illness is mad cow disease. Eating parts of infected cows can cause people to get a similar disease called Creutzfeldt-Jakob. Though cows are herbivores, they were being fed animal parts that carried the disease. Feeding them these products has now been banned.

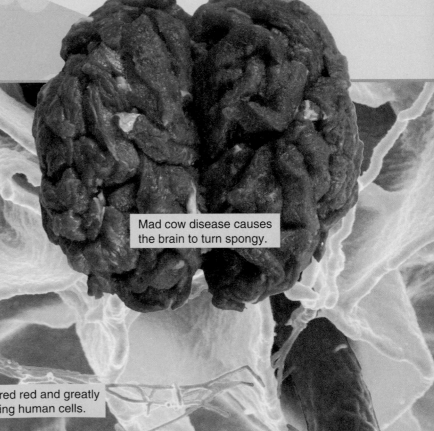

Mad cow disease causes the brain to turn spongy.

Salmonella — colored red and greatly magnified — invading human cells.

Surprise!

It's almost impossible to keep contaminants such as dirt, insect parts, and rodent hairs out of our food, but most governments do have guidelines to keep the amounts low. There's nothing appealing about rodent hairs in cereal, but some people think we should allow more insect parts in our foods. Then growers could use fewer pesticides, plus we'd get some extra nutrients!

Food Allergies

When you're allergic to a food, your body's immune system mistakenly identifies a protein as being harmful and overreacts. In extreme cases, sometimes seen with peanut and nut allergies, the immune system's reaction can be fatal. Because of this, many schools have decided the safest thing to do is to ban these foods.

The Obesity Epidemic

Since 1980, the number of obese preteens in the United States has more than doubled. The same thing is happening around the world, and it's happening to all ages. Why? For kids, it's partly because they're not getting enough exercise. But a bigger reason is that young people everywhere are surrounded by high-calorie, low-nutrient food products in fast food restaurants, at the dinner table, in advertising, and even in schools.

What You Can Do

1. **Be active every day — walk, dance, play, have fun!**

2. **Eat more vegetables, fruits, nuts, and whole grains.**

3. **Reduce the amount of sweet and fatty foods you eat.**

4. **Eat fewer animal products.**

5. **Don't skip meals or try fad diets.**

Food for Thought

There are almost seven billion people on this planet. How on Earth can there be enough...

FOOD?

What exactly are we all eating?
Where does it come from?
Is it all safe to eat?

Do we want to eat:

Animals...

...or not?

Food from close
to home...

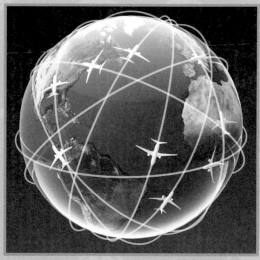

...or from far
away?

Sort-of cheese...

...or actual
cheese?

Growing Now

The way we grow food has changed enormously in the past century.

32 bpa
1906

109 bpa
1979

154 bpa
2008

bpa = bushels per acre

Fewer Farmers Growing More

A hundred years ago, the average American farmer grew a variety of crops and livestock, enough to feed his own family and 12 other people. Today, because production methods have improved so much, that same farm feeds 130 people. But now there are far fewer farmers and much larger farms. Many of these farms specialize in only one crop, a practice called monoculture.

The Green Revolution

The world managed to double its production of corn, wheat, and rice between the mid-1950s and the mid-1990s. New grains produced plentiful fat seed that ripened so quickly that two crops a year could be grown. Suddenly, places like India were growing enough to feed everyone. This was such an incredible change, it was called the Green Revolution.

But the miracle of industrialization didn't last long. The new hybrid grains needed lots of water, fertilizer, and pesticides — things that cost so much money that many farmers went into debt to pay for them. By the mid-1990s, the increase in production slowed. Water for irrigation is now running out, and in many places, the overuse of chemicals has poisoned wells and damaged the soil.

The Chemical Era

During World War II, explosives were made with ammonium nitrate. Later on, the same chemical was used to make nitrogen fertilizers. Other chemicals were developed to kill weeds and insects. All of these chemicals helped to increase the world's food supply. But problems come with their use. It takes a lot of energy to produce them. Some are so toxic, they've been banned. And runoff of fertilizers from farms creates dead zones in the world's oceans.

After World War II, munitions factories switched to making fertilizer.

Fertilizers and pesticides are sprayed on crops.

Big Machines

In 1920, there were only 225 tractors in all of the United States. Now almost all farms have tractors. But big machines like the combine are what really changed farming. Harvesting and threshing grain was once done by hand. Combines now do all the work 200 times faster, allowing farmers to own and harvest huge areas of cropland. In 1900, almost half of North Americans worked in agriculture. Now, because of machines, it's only 2 to 5 people out of a hundred!

Want to try an orple? Or is it an appange?

Playing with Genes

Scientists have figured out how to move genes from one species to another. This is called genetic modification (GM), or biotechnology. The big difference between GM foods and ones that have been selectively bred is that we can now choose a single gene from one living thing and insert it into another. We can even move genes from plants to animals! But this technology is so new that we're not yet sure how safe all GM foods are.

Scientists can now move genes between species.

Where's the Meat?

As human populations have grown, the way farm animals are raised has changed.

Each year more than a billion pigs are slaughtered around the world.

Industrial Animals

Factory farms can house 250,000 animals at a time and are designed to save money. Because disease spreads easily in such crowded conditions, antibiotics are regularly fed to the animals whether they are sick or not. None go outside. Most have no bedding. Their waste pollutes land and water. But the world wants meat — and most people don't want to pay very much for that meat.

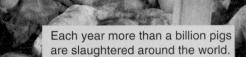

In North America, less than 2% of pigs ever get to go outside.

Bred to Grow

Though chickens can live for more than fifteen years, a typical meat bird is slaughtered when it's only a few weeks old. Egg-layers, kept in cages, are allowed to live for about a year. Almost all chickens and turkeys in North America are raised in crowded factory farm conditions because this is the cheapest way to keep them. As people become informed, more are choosing to pay extra for meat and eggs so chickens can live better lives.

8 weeks

1 day

Slaughterhouses

Slaughterhouses have grown so big that some can handle 10,000 hogs or 5,000 cattle a day. Most of the time, animals are stunned unconscious before they are bled and butchered. To avoid contamination of meat with contents of the animals' digestive systems, there are strict rules about cleanliness. But workers have to do their jobs so quickly that it's impossible to keep all the nasty bacteria off the meat.

Is Cheap Really Cheap?

Our overcrowded system of raising animals means that meat is cheap, but there are hidden costs. The animals suffer, living short lives in unnatural conditions. Our environment suffers, too — 18% of the world's greenhouse gas emissions are created by animal farming. Animal waste also poisons our land and water, and millions of people are sickened by bacteria from manure every year. If you add on the costs of other health issues, cheap meat doesn't sound quite so cheap anymore.

Most beef cattle spend their final months in crowded feedlots.

Other Meat Choices

Organic — pesticide-free feed; no medications unless sick; continuous access to outdoors; more space.

Certified Humane — animals treated humanely; given lots of space to move around; not organic.

Free Range — some access to outdoors; not organic.

Flexitarianism — eating meat only occasionally.

Vegetarianism — not eating meat at all.

Food on the Move

Most of us now rely on other people to grow our food, so food has to travel to get to us.

Bring Me Food!

For many of us, very little of the food we buy is now grown near our homes. Most is brought to us by ship, plane, rail, and truck, and is often refrigerated while it travels. Because transportation uses fossil fuels, it contributes to the environmental footprint of the food we eat. Some people want food mile labels put on products so we'll know more about what we're buying at the supermarket.

Energy for Energy

We get energy from food, but it also takes energy to get food to our tables. Agriculture uses huge amounts of fossil fuels on chemicals, machinery, and transport. Depending on where you live, the amount of energy, or calories, spent on getting lettuce to you in the winter can be more than fifty times the energy you get from eating that same lettuce!

Eat Your View!

"Eat your view" is another way of saying we should eat more locally grown food. Local food can use less fuel for transport, so it leaves a smaller environmental footprint. Because it doesn't travel far, it's usually fresher, so it tastes better and is more nutritious. Choosing food from nearby is also a great way to support the farmers in your community!

Which Tomato Would You Rather Eat?

Bred to Travel

Most fruits and vegetables we buy today are types that travel well. These aren't bred for juiciness or flavor — they're bred to produce a lot of regularly sized fruit that resist bruising. Though there are about 7,500 varieties of tomatoes in the world, you'll find only a handful of these in most grocery stores.

Whatever You Want

People everywhere now expect to eat what they want, no matter how far away it's grown or what season it is. Some foods *have* to travel, such as tropical fruits that won't grow in cold climates. But at your local grocery store, you'll find that some produce imported from far away can also be, and probably is, grown locally. Workers' wages are much lower in developing countries, so even with the added cost of transportation, produce from these places can be bought by sellers much more cheaply than local produce.

Bananas
Iceland

Squid
Japan

Smoked Reindeer
Finland

Corn
Korea

Hard-boiled Eggs
France

Refried Beans
Mexico

Pickled Ginger
India

Pizza Around the World

A good example of globalization — the growing connection of the world's markets, businesses, and ideas — is how everyone, everywhere, has embraced pizza! Most places serve a version with tomato sauce and cheese. But almost everywhere, people add their own special ingredients, like the ones shown here.

World Problems

More and more, the way we grow food is having negative effects on us, as well as on our planet.

Global Warming

Scientists believe that human-caused greenhouse gases contribute to global warming. Agriculture produces these gases in many ways, such as when fossil fuels are burned to make fertilizers and run farm machinery, or when a billion cows belch out methane gas as part of their digestive process. Global warming will also affect agriculture. Hotter summers can make grains grow faster, but too much heat reduces production. Dry parts of the world will become even drier, so we can expect more serious droughts like the recent ones in the United States, Australia, China, Argentina, and parts of Africa.

Biofuels

Partly because fossil fuel prices keep rising and partly to try to hold back global warming, the world is looking for other energy sources. One of these sources is biofuels, such as ethanol made from corn. But some of the corn that was being grown for food is now being sold to make ethanol, and the demand is rising. A rise in demand for almost anything also means a rise in prices, so the price of *all* corn has gone up.

Corporate Farms

More and more farming is being controlled by big businesses, or corporations. Sometimes farmers still own the land they farm, but what they grow, and how they grow it, is controlled by a corporation. Corporations are also buying up family farms and then hiring other people to work the land.

Who's in Charge?

Corporations also, increasingly, control the way our food moves from farm to consumer. For instance, one huge business buys grain from farmers who are under contract to work for them, then feeds that grain to factory-farmed animals. The meat is processed in factories the corporation owns, using additives it also makes. The corporation then sells the finished processed foods to grocery stores or fast food outlets. It makes money every step of the way.

The Farmers' Dilemma

1900 Farmers didn't have to buy much. Work horses made more horses. Seed was saved and planted. Animal manure fertilized fields.

2010 Farmers buy most of what they need: machinery, fuel, chemicals, seed. Newer varieties of grains even have "terminator" genes implanted in them to prevent saved seed from sprouting. The cost of all these things adds up, and it keeps rising. Unfortunately, what many farmers make on their crops isn't keeping up with what they have to spend, and they go deeper and deeper into debt.

Only One?

Monoculture is a system of growing only one type of a single crop, often on large farms. Farmers only need equipment and supplies for this one crop. Problems come up when market prices fall or these crops fail. Also, if a new disease appears and everyone is growing the same variety of crop, huge amounts of food can be wiped out. About a million people starved to death when a blight killed Ireland's potatoes in the mid-1800s. They were all the same kind of potato.

R.I.P.
Gros Michel

We almost lost the banana when a disease caused by a soil fungus killed off the export type, Gros Michel, in the 1950s. Now there's the Cavendish, but because of monoculture, the same thing could happen again.

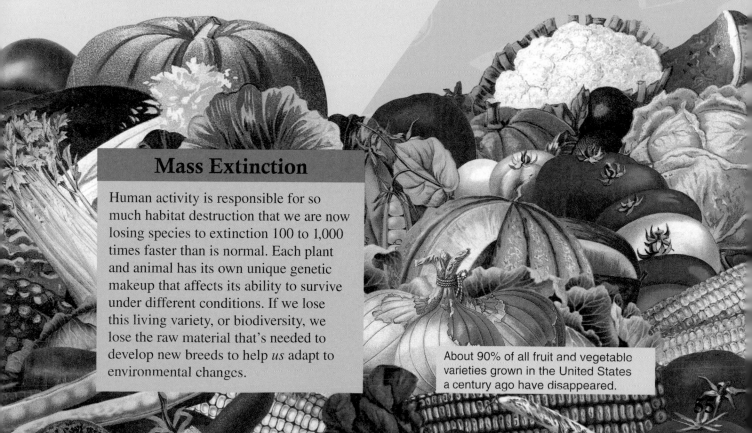

Mass Extinction

Human activity is responsible for so much habitat destruction that we are now losing species to extinction 100 to 1,000 times faster than is normal. Each plant and animal has its own unique genetic makeup that affects its ability to survive under different conditions. If we lose this living variety, or biodiversity, we lose the raw material that's needed to develop new breeds to help *us* adapt to environmental changes.

About 90% of all fruit and vegetable varieties grown in the United States a century ago have disappeared.

Feeding the World

The world grows enough food to give everyone plenty of calories each day, yet every six seconds a child dies from hunger.

1,220 calories

200 calories

6,800,000,000 Mouths to Feed

More than a billion people don't get enough to eat. Some are hungry because of drought or war. Others are simply trapped in poverty. They can't afford seed to plant, tools to work with, or an education. Sadly, while so many have so little, more than a billion adults on Earth are overweight. Right now the world has enough food for everyone, but this food is not equally shared.

人口

In Chinese, the characters for "person" and "mouth" are joined to make the word "population."

Changing Populations

Until recently more people lived in rural areas. But modern agriculture pushes small farmers off their land and into cities. In the developing world, many of these people can't find work and could end up living in crowded, unsanitary slums. Others, though, are doing well. And these people want what the developed world already has: cars, houses, laptops, and of course, meat.

About a billion people live in slums like this one in Mumbai, India.

As China prospers, its meat consumption goes way up.

Where to Farm?

Much of Europe and parts of North America were completely deforested long ago for farming. Today it's the developing world's turn, and forests are being cleared at an alarming rate in Asia, Africa, and South America. But even while new farmland is being created, we're also losing it. With today's agricultural practices, soil can become overly salty, or it erodes, or it turns into desert. Meanwhile, all over the world, huge areas of our best farmland — near where people first chose to settle — are being gobbled up by the growth of cities.

The bald uakari is just one of thousands of species threatened by forest loss.

Where Food Money Goes

In the developing world, it's normal for people to spend at least half their income on food. In rich countries, some of us spend only 10% of what we make on food — and in some places that includes what we spend in restaurants! Meanwhile, the percentage of each food dollar that goes to the farmers who grow our food gets lower every year, while the percentage that goes to corporations increases.

A quarter of a million underfed children go blind each year because of a lack of vitamin A. Golden Rice was developed to help reduce this problem. But some people think genetically modified crops like this one are a Band-Aid solution for a bigger problem. If poor people had vegetables to eat with their rice, they would get plenty of vitamin A.

Science to the Rescue?

Some people think we can solve the world's food supply problems with a new Green Revolution — this one based on growing genetically modified crops. Scientists are working on developing new varieties that are more drought resistant or heat tolerant, and others that provide more nutrients. But most research money is being spent by private companies that want to make a profit. We need our governments to invest more in research to help end world hunger.

What to Do?

Many people believe our future depends on sustainable agriculture.

What It Means

Sustainable agriculture produces food while helping to protect the environment, workers, and communities. It's based on the idea of agricultural stewardship — the careful management of our planet's resources to ensure that everyone has enough good food to eat now, and in the future.

How Sustainable Farming Works

Farmers allow animals to graze outdoors and eat crop waste. Animal manure is used to build soil fertility. More than one crop is grown, and chemical fertilizers and pesticides are avoided. Water is conserved and kept clean. Farm workers are paid decent wages.

Food is sold near where it is grown, and everyone pays a fair price for it. Governments need to support these producers, as well as their communities. And consumers also need to support them by buying locally grown, sustainable products as much as possible.

Saving Food Diversity

A global fund has recently been established to protect the world's diversity of food crops. One of the projects is a vault in Norway that already contains more than half a million seed varieties. Some rich countries have now agreed to pay farmers in poor countries to continue growing traditional varieties of such crops as potatoes that can't be stored as easily as seeds. If there's a world food crisis, which might happen with climate change, the hope is that we'll be able to develop commercial crops from these ancient varieties.

More than 250,000 strains of maize, or corn, are being kept safe in seed banks.

Peruvian farmers will be paid to look after their ancient types of potatoes.

Don't Throw It Away!

Restaurant food is left uneaten, a tub of yogurt goes moldy in your fridge, you throw half your school lunch in the garbage — these are just some of the ways that huge amounts of food are wasted. It sounds like we don't think food is valuable — but it is. We use enormous quantities of fuel and water to grow it, process it, and transport it. Not only that, but rotting food produces methane, a powerful greenhouse gas.

Up to a quarter of North America's food goes to waste!

Water

To irrigate dry places, we've tapped into ancient underground reservoirs, but many of these water sources are running low. At the same time, global warming is making seasonal rains more undependable. Water conservation must be taken seriously, even in places that still have lots of fresh water. Covering soils with mulches can help slow evaporation. Underground tanks that store rain from tropical downpours can water crops in drier times. We also need to develop new water-saving technologies, such as dew- and fog-collecting systems.

Dew- and fog-harvesting systems can supply water for irrigation in areas without a lot of rainfall.

Grow Your Own Salad!

If you have a sunny backyard, or even a balcony, it's easy and rewarding to grow some of your own food. If you can't do it at home, many cities have community gardens — spaces that a number of people share. When you grow your own vegetables, not only can you get the freshest produce possible, but also choose seeds for all kinds of varieties that you're unlikely to find at the grocery store, like Easter egg radishes, purple tomatoes, and candy-striped beets!

59

You Have Choices!

We all have to eat, but deciding *what* to eat, and feeling good about our choices, is not so easy these days. But it *can* be done.

Your Wallet = Power

Businesses make money by selling things. If no one buys what they're selling, they'll switch to selling what buyers want. It's as simple as that. Organic foods are the fastest-growing section of the food industry today because people want to buy them.

Be a Smart Consumer

Food marketers spend a lot of money studying kids. They know all about pester power — the ways kids get their parents to buy things for them. Marketers know that the bitter flavors kids don't like can be disguised with sugar and salt. And they also know that if they get kids used to eating lots of sugar, salt, and fat while they're young, that's what they'll want in foods when they grow up.

Go to the Farmer!

At farmers' markets you can buy fresh food from the same people who produce that food — people you can talk to about how they grow their carrots or make their cheese or feed their ducks. Lots of these people are so proud of the food they produce that they'll let you come to their farms to see how they do it.

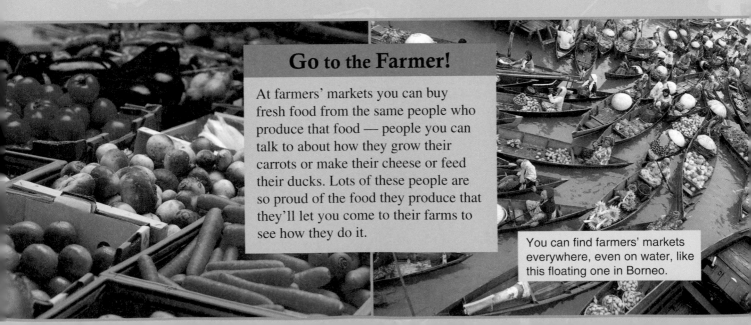

You can find farmers' markets everywhere, even on water, like this floating one in Borneo.

Learn How to Cook!

There's a good reason why processed foods are called convenience foods — they're fast and they're easy. But you might be surprised to find out how many delicious things you can whip up in the kitchen in just a few minutes with fresh ingredients. And when you're the cook, *you* get to decide what's for dinner. If you start now, there's no reason you can't be a fabulous chef by the time you're ready to leave home!

To Meat or Not to Meat

Lots of us struggle with the question of whether to eat meat, especially when we hear things about factory farms. But eating a vegetarian diet is not easy. Because we have the bodies of omnivores, if we don't eat meat we have to get some of the nutrients we need from other things. So if you want to give up meat, you'll need to learn what a healthy vegetarian diet is.

But I Really Like Sausage!

Instead of becoming full vegetarians, many people who are concerned about food issues, such as animal welfare, the environment, world hunger, and their own health, are choosing to be flexitarians — occasional meat eaters. If everyone went meatless for just one day a week, each year we would save massive amounts of fuel, water, and grain, and we'd also prevent the release of millions of tons of greenhouse gases!

Enjoy Your Pizza!

But remember, food doesn't grow on trees. Oh, wait! Yes, it does!

Since most of us live in cities and can't actually *see* where our food is grown, we sometimes forget that our food *is* grown. That fruits and vegetables and nuts and grains all come from living plants. That the meat we eat comes from what were once living, breathing animals. So go ahead — chow down on that pizza. But before you do, take a second or two to think about where that pizza came from.

Glossary

bacteria – microorganisms that get nutrients from their environment in order to survive

biodiversity – the variation of life forms in a given ecosystem

breed – to produce, or to cause to produce, by sexual reproduction

calorie – a unit used to measure energy

dominance – the ability to exercise the most influence or control

enzyme – a complex protein produced by a living organism that brings about or speeds up a chemical reaction

gene – the basic biological unit of heredity

genetic modification – any alteration of a living organism's genetic material

genetics – the branch of biology that deals with heredity

heredity – the passing on of genes and genetic characteristics from parent to offspring

microorganism – any microscopic or submicroscopic form of life

mutant – an organism that has undergone genetic mutation

mutation – a permanent change in the genetic material of a living thing

nutrient – a food or other substance that provides energy or building material to a living thing

pasteurize – the process of heating a beverage or food to kill harmful microorganisms

selective breeding – the process of breeding animals or plants with desirable characteristics with the hope that these characteristics will be passed on to offspring

Resources

The Internet is jam-packed with information about food. Here are a few interesting Web sites — and a book! Most are designed for kids. The others are easy to understand and full of fascinating information.

A big food site that includes info about world food and agriculture history, cultures, and farming practices: **www.museum.agropolis.fr/english/index.html**

An online encyclopedia of foods and ingredients: **www.practicallyedible.com/edible.nsf/pages/encyclopaedia**

An interesting site about soil: **soil.gsfc.nasa.gov**

Learn about ocean and fish issues: **www.montereybayaquarium.org/cr/seafoodwatch.aspx**

All about genetics, from heredity to cells to cloning: **learn.genetics.utah.edu/**

To find the nutritional content of various foods — vitamins, minerals, types of fat, calorie count, etc. — just type in a specific ingredient or the name of a prepared food and then click "submit": **www.nal.usda.gov/fnic/foodcomp/search/**

An extensive kids' cooking site that includes lessons on reading recipes, kitchen safety, and how to cook with lots of kid-friendly recipes: **www.kids-cooking-activities.com/index.html**

The Omnivore's Dilemma for Kids: The Secrets Behind What You Eat, Michael Pollan, Dial Books for Young Readers

Acknowledgments

The author would like to gratefully acknowledge the financial support of the Ontario Arts Council. Care has been taken to trace ownership of copyright materials contained in this book. Information enabling the publisher to rectify any reference or credit line in future will be welcomed. 6: (apple) ©istockphoto.com/Oliver Wolfson; (cow) ©istockphoto.com; (patties) ©istockphoto.com/Lauri Patterson; 7: (koala) © Jenny Rollo; (spider) Dez Pain; (shark) ©istockphoto.com/ThePalmer; (bear) ©istockphoto.com/fishfetish; (snail) ©istockphoto.com/Westergren; 9: (kneading) ©istockphoto.com/JackJelly; (sardine) ©istockphoto.com/syagci; 10: (girl) ©istockphoto.com/izusek; 11: (boy) ©istockphoto.com/ajphoto; 12: (boy) Shutterstock/Andrey Shadrin; 13: (fish skin, etc.) courtesy Frankie Thornhill; (scale insect) Whitney Cranshaw, Colorado State University, Bugwood.org; 14: (girl) Shutterstock/Kameel4u; 15: (flatbread) ©istockphoto.com/bryatta; 17: (girl) Shutterstock/Sianc (honeyguide) Alamy/FLPA; 18: (boy) Shutterstock/Paul Prescott; 20: (girl & cow) Shutterstock/Larisa Lofitskaya; (lamb) Shutterstock; (wild boar) Dreamstime; (wild sheep) Dreamstime; (horses) Dreamstime; 21: (water buffalo) ©istockphoto.com/ronen; (geese) Dreamstime; 27: (girl) Shutterstock/ Jacek Chabraszewski (TV kids) Shutterstock/Thomas M. Perkins; 29: (boy) Shutterstock/Algecireño; 34: (fisherman and halibut) National Oceanic & Atmospheric Administration; 36: (girl & cow) Shutterstock/Dan70; 37: (cheese, maggots) ©istockphoto.com; 40: (bees) courtesy Fred Gottschalk; 42: (family) ©istockphoto.com/MentalArt; 43: (boy) Shutterstock/Varina & Jay Patel; 44: (Salmonella) Rocky Mountain Laboratories, NIAID, NIH; 49: (munitions workers) Alfred T. Palmer/Library of Congress, Prints & Photographs Division, FSA/OWI Collection; 56: (boy) Shutterstock/Sam Dcruz; 59: (girl) Shutterstock/Anthony Harris; 61: (jumping kids) Shutterstock/Jacck Chabraszcwski (salad girl) ©istockphoto.com/Thomas_EyeDesign; 62: (boy) Shutterstock/Couperfield.

Index